Roses
and
Other Flower Designs

Lindsay P. Butterfield

DOVER PUBLICATIONS, INC.
Mineola, New York

Bibliographical Note

Roses and Other Flower Designs is a revised republication of the designs from the portfolio *Floral Forms in Historic Design: Mainly From Objects in the Victoria & Albert Museum But Including Examples from Designs by William Morris and C. F. A. Voysey,* first published by B. T. Batsford, Ltd., London in 1922. The plates have been reorganized and the "Preface" and "Descriptions to Plates" have been omitted. A new Publisher's Note has been written for this edition.

DOVER *Pictorial Archive* SERIES

Library of Congress Cataloging-in-Publication Data

Butterfield, Lindsay P.
    [Floral forms in historic design]
    Roses and other flower designs / Lindsay P. Butterfield.
        p.   cm. — (Dover pictorial archive series)
    A revised republication of the designs from Floral forms in historic design.
    Originally published under: Floral forms in historic design.
  London : B. T. Batsford, ltd., 1922.
    ISBN 0-486-29417-X (pbk.)
    1. Decoration and ornament—Plant forms.   I. Title.   II. Series.
  NK1560.B8   1996
  745.4—dc20   96-36599
                                                      CIP

Manufactured in the United States of America
Dover Publications, Inc., 31 East 2nd Street, Mineola, N.Y. 11501

PUBLISHER'S NOTE

The revival of interest in decorative arts in the early part of the twentieth century created an enormous demand for designs for textiles, wallpapers, lamps, pottery, furniture, clothing, etc. *Floral Forms in Historic Design,* published in 1922, was intended as a sourcebook, giving artists an overview of how plant forms, particularly roses, had been handled by artists in the past. The motifs were drawn from many different countries and from a wide variety of articles—pottery, ceramic tiles, inlaid wood, painted and lacquered wood, tapestries, damasks, brocades, etc. Most were from material in the Victoria & Albert Museum in South Kensington, London; however, in order to give an idea of how others had interpreted historic designs, some motifs were taken from the work of two British artists—William Morris, whose designs had revolutionized Victorian taste, and Charles Francis Annesley Voysey, whose designs were a source of Art Nouveau inspiration.

Each motif is identified by artist, where applicable, or by country and century.

Rose. By C. F. A. Voysey.

ROSE. 1. Flemish or Dutch, eighteenth century. 2, 3. English, eighteenth century.

ROSE. 1. Russian, eighteenth century. 2. English, eighteenth century.

ROSE. 1, 4. French, eighteenth century. 2, 3. English, late seventeenth or early eighteenth century.

4

ROSE. French, eighteenth century.

5

ROSE. By William Morris.

ROSE. By William Morris.

ROSE. Rhodian or Turkish, sixteenth century.

ROSE. Rhodian or Turkish, sixteenth century.

ROSE. Rhodian or Turkish, sixteenth century.

ROSE. Indian, seventeenth century.

ROSE. 1. Persian, seventeenth century. 2. Persian, sixteenth century. 3, 4. Indian, seventeenth century.

12

ROSE. Persian, seventeenth century.

13

ROSE. 1, 3. Indian, eighteenth century. 2. Persian, seventeenth century.

14

ROSE. Persian, eighteenth century.

15

ROSE. 1. Turkish, seventeenth century. 2. Persian, eighteenth century.

ROSE. Indian, eighteenth century.

DOUBLE ALMOND AND QUINCE. Chinese, eighteenth century.

18

DOUBLE ALMOND AND QUINCE. Chinese, eighteenth century.

19

PLUM. Chinese, eighteenth century.

ROSE. Chinese, eighteenth century.

21

ROSE. Chinese, eighteenth century.

CARNATION. English, eighteenth century.

CARNATION. 1. English, seventeenth century. 2. Flemish, sixteenth century.

CARNATION. 1, 2. Italian, seventeenth century. 3. Italian, eighteenth century.

ROSE. 1. English, seventeenth century. 2. Italian, sixteenth century.

ROSE. 1, 3. English, late sixteenth or early seventeenth century. 2. Swiss, fifteenth century.

ROSE. 1. Flemish, sixteenth century. 2. English, seventeenth century. 3. Italian, fifteenth century. 4. By C. F. A. Voysey.

28

ROSE. 1. English, seventeenth century. 2. Italian, sixteenth century.

29

1   2

3

4   5

ROSE. 1, 3, 4, 5. By C. F. A. Voysey. 2. By William Morris.

ROSE. 1, 2. English, fifteenth century. 3, 4. Italian, fifteenth century.

ROSE. 1. French, eighteenth century. 2. English, eighteenth century.

32

ROSE. English, eighteenth century.

ROSE. 1. French, eighteenth century. 2. English, eighteenth century.

ROSE. English, eighteenth century.

35

ROSE. Adapted from examples in Gerard's *Herball,* 1597.

CARNATION. Adapted from examples in Gerard's *Herball*, 1597.

ALMOND OR PEACH. Syrian, sixteenth century.

38

ALMOND OR PEACH. Syrian, sixteenth century.

39

ALMOND. 1. Persian, sixteenth century. 2, 3. Persian, seventeenth century.

40

1

2

3

ALMOND. 1, 2. Turkish, fifteenth century. 3. Persian, seventeenth century.

CARNATION. Syrian, sixteenth century.

42

CARNATION. 1. Rhodian, sixteenth century. 2, 3. Turkish, sixteenth century.

43

CARNATION. Syrian, sixteenth century.

44